LIKE MY MOTHER

ALWAYS SAID . . .

Erin McHugh

LIKE MY MOTHER

ALWAYS SAID . . .

WISE WORDS, WITTY WARNINGS, AND ODD ADVICE WE NEVER FORGET

Erin McHugh

Abrams Image

New York

Editor: David Cashion
Designer: Rachel Willey
Illustrations: Rachel Willey, Sebit Min, and Heesang Lee
Production Manager: Anet Sirna-Bruder

Library of Congress Control Number: 2013945683

ISBN: 978-1-4197-1173-2

Text copyright © 2014 Erin McHugh

Printed and bound in U.S.A.
10 9 8 7 6 5 4 3 2 1

Abrams Image books are available at special discounts when purchased in quantity for premiums and promotions as well as fundraising or educational use. Special editions can also be created to specification. For details, contact specialsales@abramsbooks.com or the address below.

115 West 18th Street
New York, NY 10011
www.abramsbooks.com

For my own mother,
and for everyone who ever had one.

"Erin McHugh, you never have a *bit* of fun."

— **DOROTHY KAVANAUGH McHUGH,** mother of Erin McHugh

"Sooner or later we all quote our mothers."

— **Philosopher BERN WILLIAMS**

CONTENTS

INTRODUCTION

Everyone has a mother. *Everyone*! And people tend to quote their moms, rely on their advice, and refer back to something they said probably more than they ever realize.

How do I know? Because that's exactly how this book came to be.

I was staying overnight with some friends, and during my visit one of them said to me, "I know what book you should work on next. Three times since you've been here, you've said, 'Like my mother always said . . .'"

I really didn't believe her. I asked her to parrot back to me what I'd said, because I never would have thought of myself as someone who quotes her mother. My mom has been gone more than twenty years now, so it's not like I would be repeating an incident from yesterday. But she ticked them all off, and I thought, Wow, I *do* do that. Without even realizing it, every day I'm leaning on, laughing at, and listening to my mom. And then I thought: What fun it would be to hear what everybody else's mother always said.

So I started asking my friends. And they asked their friends. Suddenly, I was getting quotes and stories from men and women I'd never met. Funny stuff, sad stories, touching quotes, loving anecdotes. And lots of nutty. Because how can mothers get through it all without the nutty? It became a very long parlor game of "Top this!"—and everybody wanted to play.

So here's *Like My Mother Always Said . . .* and what other people's moms have been saying. It's a little treasury so we can keep our mothers with us: the good, the bad, and the crazy. And whether your mother is long gone, like mine, or texting you forty times a day, you're going to see her here in these pages. So enjoy her.

ERIN McHUGH

September 2013
New York City

OH,
MOM!

Some things were ever thus: eye-rolling when your mother is being embarrassing, door-slamming, muttering under your breath. And the deep, deep sigh, accompanied by the universal "Oh, *Mom.*"

"NOBODY WANTS TO TALK TO YOU UNLESS YOU HAVE GEORGE WASHINGTON IN YOUR POCKET."

— **ANN,** mother of Marianne

"I am not your friend;
I am your mother."

— SUSAN, mother of Tamara

"IT'S ONLY
A PROBLEM IF
YOU MAKE IT
A PROBLEM."

— ROSEMARY, mother of Betsy

"Pain equals growth."

— BARBARA, mother of Michelle

"Oh, no thanks, I'll just
have a sip of yours."

— TESSIE, mother of Suzy

"That really gets
my Irish up!"

— NANCY, mother of Jonathan

"You're wishing your
life away."

— KAY, mother of David

"Your eyes look sick."

— DOTTIE, mother of Erin

"*I* know when you're sick."

— HAZEL, mother of Hope

"'I want, I want, I want.'
People in hell
want ice water."

— BETTY, mother of Alisa

"Somebody's gonna
end up crying."

— SWANEE, mother of Valerie

"Every woman should
have a nice gay man
looking after her."

— JO, mother of Elisa

I grew up with just my brother,
and my mother would always joke,
"I have a third child, Not Me.
Whenever I ask who did something,
my kids respond, 'Not Me!'"

— EMILY, daughter of Sally

"ASK YOUR FATHER."

— PAT, mother of Mary Claire

"You are not going out when they honk
the horn. We have a doorbell."

— ALICE, mother of Patty

My mother wrote letters to me regularly in college and always signed them, "Love, Mother," except for one time when she signed, "Kathryn, your mother." This became the dorm joke—that my mother had to *remind* me who she was. When I spoke to her about it many years later, she said that she had initially signed it as if writing to a friend, realized what she'd done, and tried to remedy it by adding "your mother." It's a plausible explanation, I suppose. But the result was that I put it on my bulletin board and loads of people got a kick out of it. She also used to send me articles from *Reader's Digest* on what she considered relevant topics, such as sex, venereal disease, drugs, and so on, all of which also went on the bulletin board. She helped to educate my entire dorm—though whether anyone took her advice is another question!

— **SUSAN,** daughter of Kathryn (her mother)

On the dangers of TV:

"That thing is the idiot's lantern."

— **VALERIA,** mother of Elisa

Whenever I would complain that one thing or another wasn't fair, Mom would shoot back: "Life's not fair!"

— **JODY,** daughter of Joyce

"You're not hungry. Your mouth is bored."

— **JOALICE,** mother of Sharon

"You kids think you're immortal."

— **KIMMEY,** mother of Ann

"Do you want it, or do you need it?"

— **DEE DEE,** mother of Kathie

My entire life—and I am likely on the back side now— when I've been with my mother and I'm set to leave her, she says, "Don't talk to strangers." No clue why.

— **SUSAN,** daughter of Elinor

"That's why they call it *work*!"

— SHAN-LI, mother of Jating

Even today, though I have had my own business and owned my own home for decades, my mother constantly says to me on the phone, "I hope you don't go in that pool by yourself. You might hit your head or get a cramp."

— DENISE, daughter of Gert

Whenever I got in trouble:
"What's wrong with you?
We're going to lose our house!"

— MICHELLE, daughter of Barbara

During a thunderstorm, when we were scared, Mom would say: "The angels are bowling."

— CYNTHIA, daughter of Tess

"*Nothing* in life is perfect."

— LOIS, mother of Janice

My mom ends every conversation with a lilting, "So that's the scoop!" Even if she just told you someone died.

— KATHLEEN, daughter of Barbara

"PUT DOWN THAT STICK— YOU'LL PUT YOUR EYE OUT!"

— KATHERINE, mother of Peter

Every single year, when it was time to have my school picture taken, my mother would say the same thing: "Try and look pleased."

— EDMÉE, daughter of Katharine

"Why do you always try to take more than you can carry? Make more than one trip!"

— ROSLYN, mother of Candice

Whenever we would ask Mom to find something we'd lost (and it would often be in plain sight), she'd say: "None so blind as he who will not see."

— ROCKY, son of Sylvia

"You're lucky you have a dishwasher to empty."

— TIMMY, mother of Lisa

My mother was a pet-name person, and while she called us by our first names often (or by one another's: "Lara, Colin, Beckie—whatever your name is"), she more often called us by sweet names. Lamb. Sweetheart. Lovie. My sweet lamb. Goose. My love. La Bean. Sweetpea. Perhaps the worst was when I was picked up by a heavy-metal heartthrob to go skating at Montvale Roller Rink; she sent me off on my date by asking, "So, what time will you be home, Meatball?" How embarrassing.

— **LARA,** daughter of Debbie

I would say to my mother, "Why didn't you ever give me any compliments?" She'd say, "I didn't want you to get a swelled head."

— Singer and actor **BARBRA STREISAND,** daughter of Diana

Mom is superstitious. When my husband and I were moving from an apartment on the tenth floor to a larger apartment on the eighth, my mother told me that I must take an upholstered (it *must* be upholstered) chair out to the street and sit in it for a few minutes. Why? Because if you are moving to an apartment on a lower floor this is a necessity. Needless to say, I told her I would, though I had no intention of actually doing it. But in the middle of the move, Mom showed up, grabbed an upholstered dining room chair, and had me sitting on the chair on a very busy sidewalk in the middle of Manhattan. It made her happy, and I can't help but think it is the reason that we are so happy in our eighth-floor apartment.

— ELISSA, daughter of Frances

My mom, who was a very dedicated, highly awarded sales associate at Lord & Taylor, has always been very candid with her loyal customers—and with me. Perhaps her dry humor was slightly less acerbic at work, but one never knows.

Three weeks after giving birth, I was trying on formal dresses when she said, "That's great . . . if you're comfortable with your upper arms."

This was nothing compared to the time I was checking out a pair of patterned jeans: "A clown! A clown would wear those pants!" And I suppose she was using some discretion when she whispered, "Does the phrase *sausage casing* mean anything to you?" I was trying on yoga pants.

Shopping with her is still a treat. We usually end up laughing to the point of tears, and I have learned that I cannot wear sleeveless dresses, I don't have the thighs for patterned jeans, and I resent yoga clothing. Without her I'd have made hundreds of fashion mistakes.

— MERLE, daughter of Toni

"This will become a jewel of your crown in heaven."

— **RUTH,** mother of Faith

The end to her every conversation, no matter the subject:
"I don't know what else I can tell you."

— **DORICE,** mother of Ellen

"I don't know. Who knows, you know?"

— **BARBARA,** mother of Kathleen

"Look it up." We thought we should even have this etched on her tombstone. She would never give us the answer to anything. We had to "look it up." So annoying. Yet, after my mother died, the one thing my daughter wanted to remind her of Grandma was my mother's much-used, nearly falling apart dictionary.

— **ANNE,** daughter of Patsy

To the butcher, every single time:
"Make it a *nice* chicken."

— **ANNE,** mother of Karen

**My mom would say,
"I may be responsible for
all of your problems,
but you are responsible
for all the solutions."**

— **ANNE,** daughter of Mary Anne

On how to describe and recount dreams:
"How would you describe your
dream to a Martian?"

— **PEG,** mother of Andrew

LOVE, SEX, & MARRIAGE

"Always do this." "Never do that." "Men like," "Women hate," "No one wants". . . if it's anything mothers have endless advice on, it's your love life. Of course, it's annoying how often they're right.

"DON'T BE IMPRESSED BY A MAN'S CAR— HE MAY BE LIVING IN IT."

— CAROLYN, mother of Melody

"If the sex doesn't start out good, it's rarely going to get much better."

— **MARY LEE,** mother of Susan

"Pay attention to how a date treats the waitstaff in a restaurant. The way he treats them is how he will eventually treat you."

— **ANN,** mother of Lynn

"The only reason a woman should get married is when she can't pay the credit card bill."

— **ELSA,** mother of Mercedes

"When I want something and your father doesn't agree, I have to make him think he's right. But it plants a seed. Then he thinks it's his idea, and I get what I want!"

— **ANNE,** mother of Jen

My mother would *harrumph* when a friend got engaged to someone she didn't approve of. "There is many a slip between the cup and the lip," she'd say, meaning lots can happen before you ever reach the altar.

— **NANCY,** daughter of Roxy

"Never let your husband know
how much you can do,
because he'll let you do it."
— CARRIE, mother of Deborah

"I'm going to show your boyfriends
your room and when they see what a
slob you are, no one will marry you."
— GERALDINE, mother of Jayne

"FIND SOMEONE
WITH A BRAIN."
— JOAN, mother of Tara

"Just go out on a date with him—
you don't have to *marry* him."
— JOAN, mother of twins Martha and Sally

When we went to lunch my mother always asked the hostess for a table in the corner because, she would confide, "We have secrets to share," which meant a long, intimate conversation with her two daughters and their best friend about daily life, stories from my mother's childhood, and funny observations about the day we had just shared.

— **BUFFY,** daughter of Middy

"FRENCH KISSING IS THE STEP BEFORE SEX!"

— **CAROLE SUE,**
mother of Jennifer

On trying to cement a new relationship, my mother always advised: "For every two phone calls, you call once."

— Matchmaker **PATTY STANGER,**
daughter of Rhoda

"Marriage is not a gift dropped in your lap."

— **MARIAN,** mother of Pauline

"There's plenty of time for those kinds of things."

— **KAY,** mother of David

Advice to a woman whose engagement has been broken off:

"Never give back a diamond."

— **TILLY,** mother of Sessalee

When I was a young girl, and college still seemed like a place for girls to find husbands, my mother taught me that the best answer to the question, "What do you want to be when you grow up?" was, "Independently wealthy."

— **JOAN,** daughter of Mari

"Avoid sleeping with your male friends or you won't have any."

— **MARGARET,** mother of Andrea

"You're just like your Aunt Patricia—you'll sleep with anyone who says you're beautiful."

— **GLORIA,** mother of Joe

On the occasion of her daughter's marriage:
"Always keep your own money."

— **LEIGH,** mother of Gina

ON MARRIAGE: "PICK YOUR BATTLES."

— **LORETTA,** mother of Kalen

I have to say that I have not often asked my mom for advice (thinking that I always knew better, probably!), but I do remember one time I did just that. It was right before I was getting married, and I asked for her best marriage advice. She said quite simply and promptly, "Don't try to change him." At the time I didn't think much of it. But now, with my father deceased for five years, my parents married for fifty-plus years before that, and my husband and I a few years short of our own twenty-fifth wedding anniversary, I see the wisdom in her comment: What you see is what you get.

— **CAROL,** daughter of Elvira

My sister and I were about eighteen or so, and our mum, who was very English, and an English teacher, was talking to us about relationships while stirring the gravy for dinner one night.

She said in her cut-glass accent, "Well, dears, you get either the sex or the personality, but you seldom get both." My sister and I looked at each other, dumbfounded, because apart from having given us a very clear outline of the facts of life, we hadn't heard much otherwise in terms of relationship advice. That and the fact that we were desperately trying not to figure out if our father had won on sex or personality.

— **ALISON,** daughter of Audrey

"It's better to be a rich man's darling than
a poor man's slave."

— GERALDINE, mother of Jayne

On the game of young love: "Play it cool."

— SANDRA, mother of Abbe

"If you buy a man a watch, your time will run out."

— ELLA, mother of May

"Green on Monday, sex on Sunday."

— LYNN, mother of Alicia

"You should always have a set of pink sheets because
you look so much better in bed the next morning."

— JANE, mother of Ann

"The best birth control is a dime held
tightly between the knees."

— JOAN, mother of Susan

> *"It's good to get your first marriage over with."*

— **LEE,** mother of Lesley

> "There are good girls and fast girls. You do not want to be thought of as a fast girl."

— **OLIVE,** mother of Olive

> *"If you marry for money, you earn every penny."*

— **POTSIE,** mother of Stacy

I informed my parents that I would be spending the summer living on the Cape with six boys and one other girl, so they sent me a plane ticket to come home immediately. That was when I got the speech that if I slept with my boyfriend, I would be ruining "the most beautiful night of my life." (It was way, way too late for that.) When that selfsame boyfriend came home with me to meet the parents the next spring, my mother cornered him and told him, "A woman is like a bird; she needs a nest." She didn't quite say, "Marry her, or else," but evidently he got the picture.

— **ANNE,** daughter of Anne

OUCH!

Who knows how to get to you better—and faster—than your mother? The Queen of the Zinger always knows how to hit you where you live.

> "THERE ARE THOUSANDS OF OPPORTUNITIES TO KEEP YOUR MOUTH SHUT. USE THEM."

— **ELEANOR,** mother of Dianne

"If you don't remember what
you wanted to say, it couldn't have
been very important."

— EDITH, mother of Edith

"YOU HAVE CHAMPAGNE
TASTE ON A BEER INCOME."

— VIRGINIA, mother of Meredith

"No one is paying as much attention to
you as you pay to yourself."

— JOALICE, mother of Sharon

"I don't care if you get Cs, as long
as you're learning. But I'll probably be
pissed about it a little later."

— MARY, mother of Isabelle

"Do *not* make me get the wooden spoon!"

— JANICE, mother of Mary

"Life is about doing things you don't want to do."

— MARY, mother of Nancy

"I don't care who started it, I'm finishing it now!"

— HELEN, mother of John

Whenever my siblings and I started squabbling, it was always: "Love, or a hit in the head."

— ROCKY, son of Sylvia

"He touts his knowledge *summa cum loudly*."

— MARY ALICE, mother of Diane

"Suck it up, Buttercup!"

— CINDY, mother of Christine

ME: "What's for dinner?"
MOM: "D'overs."
(pause) "Leftovers."

— DOROTHY, mother of Ann

"IF YOU'VE NEVER BEEN HATED BY YOUR CHILD, YOU'VE NEVER BEEN A PARENT."

— ACTOR BETTE DAVIS, mother of Barbara

On her son's boyfriend:
"He is my cross to bear."

— JEAN, mother of Michael

"Once the water is contaminated, it's very hard to purify."

— ELEANOR, mother of Dianne

"Classy people never use the word *classy*."

— **KATHERINE,** mother of Katherine

I was practicing the piano aimlessly while my mother was in the bath. She came out, looking like a damp million bucks, and said, "If you come near a tune, play it, dear."

— **ROBERT,** son of Eleanor

"It's not who you are that counts, it's who you know."

— **BROOKS,** mother of Pamela

My mom, an Irish Tiger Mom through and through, stressed studying above all else. In addition to, "Never mind the boys, keep your mind on the books!" she also used to say, "If you get an F, just keep walking." As in, just keep walking 'cause you're not coming into my house with an F!

— **ALISON,** daughter of Beth

I don't want to say my mother had a specific favorite saying, but I will say that at her ninetieth birthday party we had cocktail napkins printed up that read: "I NEVER PROMISED YOU A ROSE GARDEN."

— **FAYE,** daughter of Mary

My mother had an entire theory—based on fruit—about the women in our family. "The apple doesn't fall far from the tree. My mom was a Granny Smith apple, tart and crisp and made a great apple pie. Your sister is a Honey Crisp, sweet and always ready for lunch. You, my dear, are a Red Delicious, good-tasting, but your skin is a bit tough and hard to swallow."

— **JULIE,** daughter of Dottie

As I would be flitting around the house, trying to work out an improvisational dance: "That's *almost* a skill."

— KAREN, daughter of Lorraine

As a lead-in when she had bad news to deliver, my mom always opened with this, figuring it sounded way worse than whatever it was she was going to tell me: "You're a big girl, it's a cruel world, and there's no Santa Claus."

— LILY, daughter of Cecelia

"Robin Carol, you would rather lie than tell the truth!"

— JENNY, mother of Robin

"She's as crazy as a road lizard."

— TILLY, mother of Sessalee

"Ooooh, I'm so full I feel like a rubber band around a watermelon!"

— LOU ANN, mother of Mary Dawn

"There's always going to be someone smarter than you, richer than you, and better looking than you. So don't get too full of yourself."

— MARILYN, mother of James

When I tried to convince my mom to let me have my way: "I understand what you're saying. I'm simply not interested."

— SUSAN, daughter of Sally

"NEVER TRUST A MAN."

— ELEANOR, mother of Denise

"You're my son and I love you, but
I don't like you very much right now."

— **GINNY,** mother of Todd

Every time my mother saw me, whether
she was greeting me at an airport or as
I was pulling into the driveway,
she always said four things:

1. "I wish you'd put on some lipstick."
2. "I wish you'd stand up straight."
3. "I wish you'd stop making those faces."
4. "Have you been to the dentist lately?"

— **HILARY,** daughter of Bertha

"Intellectual giant, emotional dwarf."

— **ROSEMARY,** mother of Dee Dee

To her son's boyfriend, every Christmas:
"If it's the Holiday Inn you're looking for, this ain't it!"

— **PEGGIE,** mother of Chris

"Don't put a razor where the hair don't grow."

— **SATYRA,** mother of Sonia

When my sisters and I were young—around ten—
we used to like getting all gussied up in our dresses
and shiny shoes (city girls!). My mom would say,
"You girls are about as sexy as a wet sneaker."
I still think about it today whenever I'm getting
ready for an occasion.

— **LISA,** daughter of Mary

From the "Sorry, it's a little too late" department:
"Don't go out with girls."

— **OLGA,** mother of Manuela

"My sons think a screwdriver is for screwing things up."

— **MARY ALICE,** mother of Gail

"Are you really going to wear *those* shoes
with *that* dress?"

— **EDITH,** mother of author Susan Orlean

"YOU'RE LAUGHING NOW?
YOU'LL BE CRYING SOON."

— **SARA,** mother of Michael

"She could strike up a conversation
with a mannequin."

— **MARY ALICE,** mother of Lesa

"Why don't I stick the broom up my @*#
and sweep the floor while I'm at it?"

— **ELEANOR,** mother of Bill

"What did you expect? She's common."

— **ETHEL,** mother of Sara

"We were all born to die."

— **ISABEL,** mother of Karen

I know we all heard it as kids whenever we were going somewhere fun and getting more and more out of control: "Don't make me turn this car around!" I guess it finally had to happen. My mom was taking my twin brother, Jerry, and me and a bunch of our friends to the local amusement park for our birthday party, and after a couple of threats, she actually did it.

She turned the car around.

It certainly had the desired effect; silence reigned in the "way back" of the station wagon. And yes, after a mile or two she relented and headed back to the park, but I can tell you, from that moment on, it was one well-behaved party.

— **MARIE,** daughter of Mary

"Do that again and I will rip your arms and legs off and hit you over the head with the bloody stumps. Really."

— **FELICE,** mother of Shelley

FAMILY RELATIONS

It's a delicate balance, a family, and there's only room on the podium for one conductor. And I think you know who she is.

To her son as he moves back in after college:

"HOW CAN WE MISS YOU IF YOU WON'T GO AWAY?"

— JOAN, mother of Simon

"First rule of life: Don't scare your mother."

— MEGAN, mother of Cordelia

"Yours is not to wonder why, yours is just to do or die."

— JANE, mother of Ann (paraphrasing a line from Tennyson's "The Charge of the Light Brigade")

"Don't forget me" is what my mother said to me over and over in the last year of her life when she was dying at the age of thirty-three and I was eight years old. I've spent my life trying not to.

— Author KEVIN SESSUMS, son of Nancy Carolyn

"If you're good, I'll leave you all of my jewelry." This was always very compelling, as I have four sisters.

— JULIE, daughter of Eileen

"You will miss me when I'm gone."

— JUNE, mother of Patty

"IF YOU BUNGLE RAISING YOUR CHILDREN, I DON'T THINK WHATEVER ELSE YOU DO WELL MATTERS VERY MUCH."

— First Lady JACQUELINE KENNEDY ONASSIS, mother of Caroline and John

"Every mother should have a practice baby to learn on."

— BERTA, mother of Trina

I guess most of my major injuries happened on weekends or in the early evenings when my dad, Greg, would be home. I know the compound fracture of both bones in my forearm happened at that time, because after taunting a neighborhood nemesis, Joey, who had been called in for dinner, I was standing outside his house on the seat of my bike and suddenly realized I was falling. Since I knew I was an eight-year-old superhero, I dove; then I almost threw up when I saw both of the bones actually sticking out of my arm. But I picked myself up and went home. When my mother saw me, she screamed, "Jesus, Mary, and Joseph . . . GREGGGG!!!" Here's the thing— I guess we caused more trouble than I remember because I heard that a lot and was twelve before I realized that there weren't four people in the Holy Trinity.

— **MARTHA,** daughter of Eileen

After birthing eleven kids,
my mother often could be heard to say,
"Boring is beautiful."

— **DUANE,** son of Mary Alice

At the end of March, the cold nights and
warm days create a pulse in sugar maples
that enables Vermonters to insert a tube for
"tapping" or drawing out the sap. In the 1960s,
we were often on spring vacation ski trips
when the maple-sugaring season started.
Along the roadside, tin buckets were pinned to
the trees like skirts. As the sap started to drip
out, it hit the empty tin with a ping or a pang
and a plop. My mother (who was usually the
driver) would pull to the side, jump out with
us, and bring us right up to the bucket.
Then she would say with delight,
"Listen. . . . Sap music!"

— **MARGOT,** daughter of Marion

A litany about waiting on your children:

"Are your legs painted on?
Well, then go get it yourself."

"If you don't like it, you can have
cereal and sit in the other room."

"What's for dinner?
'Make it yourself,' that's what."

"I'm not your slave."

"The kitchen is closed."

— FAITH, mother of Ruthie

My mother has been gone many years, but so many of her sayings are with me still. I had four little brothers and was the BIC (Babysitter-in-Chief), much to my impatient dismay. My mother, distracted by household chores, would suddenly say, "Go see what those kids are doing and tell them to stop."

Another one of her favorite sayings, with which I am often forced to agree, was, "Little children are not fit company for adults."

As a party girl dating back to the repeal of prohibition, she counseled, "Learn to drink anything, dear. You never know what they might be serving."

As to housekeeping: "Never get a dish dirty unless you absolutely have to."

And on and on. She was beautiful and adorable and headstrong, which led her to turn most of her life into a god-awful mess in too many ways. She married two disastrously inappropriate guys before marrying the first man she was really crazy about. Number three was also in every way the wrong guy. But he was the only one she really loved. He was handsome and gifted but utterly feckless. She thereby plunged us—herself and the two kids she already had—into poverty and promptly had three more children, which did not alleviate the situation.

We had a very messy and disorganized childhood, but I look back and wish I could recover just one hour of it. I think of her every day.

PERSONAL HYGIENE &

GOOD HEALTH

It's not just about wearing clean underpants: Moms seem to have a plethora of crazy ideas about how to keep us in tip-top shape. Not that they'll stop worrying anyway.

"ONLY TWO THINGS COUNT AT THE END OF THE DAY: YOUR HEALTH AND YOUR GOOD NAME."

—ANNIE, mother of Doris

"Don't drink your calories."

— **PAM,** mother of Maya

It was always, "Be careful, you'll eat yourself sick!" But truly, I can't remember a single person in my family who ever did.

— **LORI,** daughter of Bernie

On the occasion of a stomach virus:
"Think of how much weight you're losing."

— **THERESA,** mother of Mary

MY MOTHER TOLD ME THAT IF I PICKED MY NOSE I'D MAKE IT BIGGER.

— **MICHAEL,** son of Martha

"GO OUTSIDE. HOUSEWORK WILL WAIT— THE SUN WILL NOT."

— **EILEEN,** mother of Noreen

"*Ptu, ptu, ptu!*" Those are the three pretend spits that my mother always uses to ward off the evil eye.

— **NANETTE,** daughter of Annie

"If you grind your teeth, you have worms."

— **JACQUI,** mother of Jen

"If you go to bed with wet hair, you'll get pneumonia."

— **SHAN-LI,** mother of Jating

Mom is of the generation and social group that tend to believe appearances are everything. Thus, the way we looked was always more important than just about anything else. I remember her always reminding us to wear clean underwear because "you never know." I was never so happy to have followed this advice than when I found myself hit by a car and splayed out in the middle of 96th Street in Manhattan with my undies most definitely visible to all present—they were indeed "clean," and I was very grateful for her advice.

— **LISA,** daughter of Bobbie

When we were at dinner and had bits of food on
our faces, Mom always said, "You have a gazelle in
the garden." It was, for both of my parents,
a polite way of telling us to wipe our mouths.
The origin of this? Apparently, my mom's father had
a beard, and when her mom would spot food in it,
this was her gentle prodding to clean up.

— **DORSEY,** daughter of Jean

"Don't take any goofballs!"
my mother always said. I think
she meant drugs, but frankly,
I don't know if *she* even knew what
she meant. She was adorable.

— Cartoonist **MICHAEL MASLIN,**
son of Alberta

"Little boys should be kept in their playpens
until they are old enough to stand up and ask
directions to the men's room."

— **POLLY,** mother of Gay

" There are three ways a lady can pick
her teeth at dinner:
1. Wait until after dinner
2. Excuse herself from the table
3. Not at all"

— OLIVE, mother of Olive

On her prodigious housekeeping skills:
"The dust doesn't have time to
settle in this house."

— CLAIRE, mother of Mark

"Whenever you pass

a bathroom, go.

You can always do

a little something."

— ALMA, mother of Richard

"You are giving me a headache."
— **NOREEN,** mother of Michael

My petite mom wears a bikini at sixty. Her secret? "Eat whatever you want, but only half." Annoying when she nibbles on a box of chocolates half at a time for days, but a fun (and cheap) lunch date.
— **DEIRDRE,** daughter of Consuelo

"Gum-chewing girls are like cud-chewing cows."

— **LOLLY,** mother of Dini

I think it was the fact my mom was the mother of
five children, twelve grandchildren, and four
great-grandchildren that made her say, "I shower to
stay clean, not to *get* clean."

— **MAUREEN,** daughter of Rosemarie

"NEVER GO TO BED WITH YOUR MAKEUP ON."

— **EILEEN,** mother of Julie

You know how when you were a little kid, you never
really thought you were dirty, and so could never
understand why your mother was so horrified when
you raced in the door at the end of a tough day
of playing? When my mom would say, as she was
scrubbing away at me later on in the tub, that
I was so filthy she could grow potatoes in my ears,
I thought it was because we were Irish.

— **ERIN,** daughter of Dottie

My family was very much of the "Just let it run its course" philosophy when it came to treating childhood illnesses. Going to the doctor was something we did only to get vaccinations or if we clearly had a broken bone or something equally dramatic (like possible rabies—yes, I jest you not). Something as routine as a violent stomach virus merely prompted a plastic bucket next to my bed and my mother's "gentle and loving" admonition, "DON'T MISS!" To this day, when either my sister or I is ill, each of us is quick to jokingly remind the other, "DON'T MISS!"

— **AMY,** daughter of Tinker

UNCONDITIONAL LOVE

Is there someone else in the world who thinks we're prettier, handsomer? Who believes in our brilliance and breathtaking charm? That we'll grow up to achieve miracles? No, sadly, there is not.

"I'D SAW OFF MY OWN ARM FOR YOU."

— **TERI,** mother of author Brad Meltzer

"That is no one's pretty child,
but I am sure he is loved."

— MARTHA, mother of Betsy

My mother is an amazing listener,
and that's taught me how to listen to
my own daughters. Sometimes we
don't always want advice, just an open
ear and a big hug.

— First Lady MICHELLE OBAMA, daughter of Marian

"There's a whole lotta love in
a bowl of pasta."

— ANTOINETTE, mother of Frank

My mother said to me, "If you are a soldier, you will become a general. If you are a monk, you will become the Pope." Instead, I was a painter, and became Picasso.

— Artist **PABLO PICASSO**, son of Maria

Whenever as a kid I got caught coming in late, my mother would always say the same thing. "I was so worried," she'd yell, half-furious, half-relieved. "I was about to call the state police!" That's when you knew you were really in trouble, when she was ready to call the *state* police.

— **LEO,** son of Tessie

"Why give them the satisfaction of letting them know they hurt you? You go have the best time without them. *That* will teach them!"

— **DENISE,** mother of Alexandra

"DON'T EVER LET ANYONE DEFINE YOU; YOU DEFINE YOURSELF."

— **SHIRLEY,** mother of Tim

If she saw me hurt about anything, my mother would say: "Who cares? Ignore them, and go to bed."

— **LIZ,** daughter of Regina

A case in which a mother said nothing: One of Mum's most generous gifts to me was not telling me that she hated it when I moved to San Francisco after college until many years later, long after I had returned to the East Coast and was close to her again.

— **SU,** daughter of Marjorie

In my very early twenties, I moved back home for a couple of years. I would come in late and my mother would announce that dinner was done and I could have leftovers or find myself something to eat. If I would say, "I'm not hungry," she would say I could suit myself. Five minutes later, she would ask why I wasn't eating. When I reminded her that I was not hungry, she would say I was not doing her any favors by eating. Five minutes later, she would ask me what I wanted—and then she would make it herself.

— **RICHARD,** son of Thea

When a daughter's lost love got
his comeuppance:
"The tables turn!"

— BARBARA, mother of Kathleen

Upon going out for the day, my mother
would slip me two five-dollar bills
and say, "Take two; they're small."

— ROBERT, son of Eleanor

"The great thing about having a bunch
of kids is that they just remind you
that you're the person who takes
them to go poop. That's who you are."

— Actor ANGELINA JOLIE, mother of Maddox, Zahara,
Shiloh, Pax, Knox, and Vivienne

My mother would help you and feed you to death if she could. You can tell her that, no, I don't want one more jot of something, but it doesn't matter. One morning she finally flooded my father's cereal after he told her that he was all set. The result is that she now has personalized license plates that read, "MO MILK."

— **VERONICA,** daughter of Mare

"Who deserves it more than us?"

— **EILEEN,** mother of Ann

The truth is, it's what she doesn't say and the way she doesn't that impresses the hell out of me. She's held on to so many of her fears, annoyances, and preferences to let me figure myself out but still somehow guided me all the way and gave me the confidence to throw myself into the unknown. She's good.

— **JAY,** son of Nancy

It wasn't as much what my mom said so what she did. Mom had supreme faith in her husband, her children, her home, and her God. She wasn't a "writer," but she wrote every day, keeping a journal that chronicled what happened to her and her family in life and at home.

Mom believed in the benefit of the doubt and giving everyone a chance—or at least a chance to explain. And she was forgiving enough to allow the comfort for you to return. There was always a place at her table to have something to eat and a chance to talk.

So I would have to say it is how my mother lived, and not what she said, that spoke volumes to me—then and to this day. I hope I'm listening now.

— TOM, son of Pat

My mother had just given me a Toni Home Permanent—a big deal back in the 1960s—and it was a frizzled disaster. Plus, my daily wardrobe included wearing braces and orthopedic shoes. Needless to say, the permanent was the last straw … I thought.

But then, as I was boarding the school bus the next morning, nearly in tears, she shouted out the front door so the whole bus could hear, "You look just like Jackie Kennedy!"

— **SUSAN,** daughter of Sue

"YOU CAN DO ANYTHING YOU PUT YOUR MIND TO."

— **DORETHA,** mother of Shantelle

"Hello, darling, it's your mother."
"Hi, Mom!"
"Are you in front of that machine?"
"Yes, Mom, I'm in front of the computer most of the day."
"Well, that sounds simply dreadful—
but since you're in front of it now, I was wondering
if you could Googlize something for me."
"Sure, Mom, always happy to Googlize for you."

— **LORRAINE,** daughter of Patti

"Never forget that you are all right."

— **ISOKO,** mother of artist Yoko Ono

"IF I DIDN'T CARE ABOUT YOU, I WOULDN'T SAY ANYTHING."

— **IRMA,** mother of Jeri

I love my mother for all the times she said absolutely nothing. Thinking back on it all, it must have been the most difficult part of mothering she ever had to do: knowing the outcome, yet feeling she had no right to keep me from charting my own path.
I thank her for all of her virtues but mostly for never once having said, "I told you so."

— Author **ERMA BOMBECK,** daughter of Erma

"THEY AREN'T WORTH THE DIRT UNDER YOUR SHOES."

— **HELEN,** mother of Barbara

I broke up with someone after many years together and lived in a major slump after it happened. Shortly after the breakup, I went home for Thanksgiving and my mother—wise, all-knowing, passionate, Italian, in Palazzo pants and a blowout—took extra-special care of me throughout the day: a knowing nod, allowing me to snag a stuffed mushroom before she served them, a reprieve from garbage duty.

At the end of the night, as I gathered my stuff to head home, my mother grabbed me, brought me outside, handed me a cigarette, and lit it. We smoked together in the cold, New Jersey quiet, frozen snow on the ground, the front steps cold under our feet. Finally, she looked at me, her eyes teary, and said, "Take care of yourself. And f*ck everything else." And with that she stubbed her cigarette out under her ballet flat and kissed me good-bye.

— FRANCESCO, son of Rochelle

When I was in middle school and subjected to mean-girl banter on a daily basis, I would come home from school confused and hurt.
My mother would always say, "People are going to talk. You march right through the middle of the pack of them with your head up, shoulders straight, and never, ever let them see you sweat."

— DENISE, daughter of Connie

"Everything's going to be all right, Lovie."

— CYNNIE, mother of Cathy

When I was about to leave my first lover after several years, my mother said, "He's a good man. You know what you have, but you don't know what you're going to get."

— FRANK, son of Antoinette

My childhood did not suffer from traditional advice but rather from prolonged social coaching and insight into emotional intelligence that I, on the Asperger's spectrum, lacked spectacularly.

I had learned at a very early age that one does not go down on the floor, bark, and crawl under a table when greeted by an adult but looks the adult in the eye and shakes his or her hand. My mother is keenly emotionally and intellectually intelligent, but above all, she retains a gift for understanding what makes people tick, a subject that I had zero interest in when young. Better still, she was able to couch this understanding in terms that I could understand. When girls bullied me in middle school, she explained not that girls were bitchy and competitive but that they were like hurt, wild animals that might lash out at anything kind and different. "Don't let anyone be mean to you—that's never OK," she would say. My mother is my advocate, teacher, ally, prod, and example, and, hopefully, I can emulate her wisdom when I choose to raise offspring of my own.

— **ALI,** daughter of Barb

When I think of my mom—more than anything else . . .
more than anything—I think of the pure, immeasurable,
almost crazy love she had for me. I remember the first
time I gave her *The Tenth Justice*. It's my first published
book. My first time ever putting real work out for anyone
to see. I was terrified when she said she'd finished it.
And then she looked right at me and said, "Bradley,
I know I'm your mother, but I have to be honest with you.
This book . . . *is the greatest book of all time!*"

— Author BRAD MELTZER, son of Teri

"What I would like to give my daughter is freedom. And this is
something that must be given by example, not by exhortation.
Freedom is a loose leash, a license to be different from your
mother and still be loved. . . . Freedom is . . . not insisting that
your daughter share your limitations. Freedom also means
letting your daughter reject you when she needs to and come
back when she needs to. Freedom is unconditional love."

— Author and feminist ERICA JONG,
mother of Molly

No one expects to have their first baby be premature, let alone a preemie who was colicky for the first three months of his life and cried day and night unless he was nursing. I was fortunate, however, as my mom, who *loves* babies, lived nearby and would often wrap that baby up tight in his blanket, hold him on her lap, rub his back, and rock him for hours on end. This allowed me a shower here, a trip to the market there, and even occasional time to breathe. It kept me sane.

Still, after weeks of this, when ending her holding/rocking session, she would sometimes shake her head and say, "If he were mine, I would slip him a Mickey."

A *what?*

In complete frustration one day, I finally (and probably rudely) said, "WHAT IS A MICKEY?!?! WHERE DOES ONE GET A MICKEY??!!" The look on her face was priceless.

Of course, the truth is, she was better than any Mickey Finn in the world. Still is.

— MIMI, daughter of Tessie

My amazing mother was never one to repeat homespun edicts, but she definitely had a way of imprinting her life views when I was young. The following quote is a distillation of the kind of lesson that was offered.

"You can do anything," she might say. "If you work really hard and stay positive and just apply yoursel . . . wait, what's that on your hand? That mole looks a little dark. It might be cancer—we need to get that checked out."

Yes, growing up I learned that anything was possible, including your imminent demise.

— **DAVID,** son of Sue Lynne

KEEPING UP APPEARANCES

Sometimes having a mother is like having a human Geiger counter who detects dirt, bad taste, and poor deportment. And no, it will never stop.

"YOU LIKE WHAT YOU'RE WEARING?"

— **EDITH,** daughter of Edith

"Always polish your silver before you put it away."

— DORIS, mother of Jane

My mom found a tricky way to save money during my clothes-obsessed formative years, and it worked like a charm over and over again. She was an excellent seamstress, so whenever I'd finally convince her to take me shopping for new clothes she would inevitably exclaim, "Why I could make that for half that price—let's go get the fabric!" At which point we would leave the store and drive to the local fabric shop where she would spend a couple of dollars on fabric and a pattern and we'd head home— me, thoroughly (and mistakenly) convinced I was on the verge of a hot new outfit. For a few weeks after, Mother would claim she'd start sewing "soon"—probably (and correctly) counting on me to forget all about her promise, thanks to tons of other teenage distractions.

— AMY, daughter of Tinker

> # "I WON'T HAVE A DAUGHTER WITH GRAY HAIR."

— **JANE,** mother of Ann

When I was a teenager, every single time I came down the stairs to go out, my mother would say—from the next room and without lifting her eyes from the newspaper—"Go back upstairs and put on a bra." Certain proof that mothers have eyes in the back of their heads.

— **SUZY,** daughter of Tessie

"Sweep into the center of the room to keep the good luck in."

— **GIT JING,** mother of William

"NEVER WEAR HEELS WITH SHORTS. YOU'LL LOOK LIKE A STREETWALKER."

— **MERRILL,** mother of Sarah

"Don't ever leave the house without makeup— you never know when you're going to run into an old boyfriend."

— **NANCY,** mother of Jill

On hair care: "You look like a busted mattress."

— **CARLOTA,** mother of Poo

"Polish your shoes."

— **MARTHA,** mother of Sam

I can't tell you how many times as an adult I've visited my mother, and after a welcoming hug, she's given me the once-over and said, "Well, aren't you wearing your hair just the way you like it?"

— **ANNIE,** daughter of Sandra

It was the 1970s, obviously. Because every time I arrived home from college, my mother gave me five dollars and told me to go to Wannamaker's and buy a bra.

— **SUSAN,** daughter of Kathryn

"Your shoes should match your purse."

— **RUTH,** mother of Faith

"You don't have to buy everything that looks good on you."

— **LEE,** mother of Lesley

When my sister and I were young, and both not very interested in cleaning our rooms, our mother would constantly say, "Your rooms look like the wreck of the Hesperus." We never knew what this meant, and being children, just assumed it couldn't be good. We had heard our grandmother and great-grandmother use the phrase as well, and we knew that the Hesperus must have been quite a disaster if the state of our bedrooms were any indication.

Only years later, after hearing our mother use it in regard to her grand-children's playroom, did we question what the Hesperus actually was. She explained that it came from a poem by Longfellow about a shipwreck that ends with a young girl being found dead after the wreck, bound to the ship's mast.

So, by comparison, we figure we had it easy.

— **WILLIAM,** son of Evelyn

> ## "The living room should be as clean as if *House & Garden* is coming to photograph."

— **ELEANOR,** mother of Dianne

"Jewish girls don't camp, get their hair wet in the pool, or wear false eyelashes when it's going to rain or snow."

— **MARCIA,** mother of author Julie Klam

> ## *"Always look attractive."*

— **ROSE-ANNA,** mother of Claire

GOOD ADVICE

It's a funny thing about advice: It doesn't always seem so good when you're on the receiving end. But it sits there, and you ruminate and chew on it, and finally, the wisdom inevitably shines through.

"NEVER GO TO BED MAD."

—DOTTIE, mother of Erin

"If you don't like it, change it."

— MARTHA, mother of Sue

"If fish kept his mouth shut, he would not get hooked."

— EILEEN, mother of Juliet

"Use it up, wear it out, make it do, or go without."

— MARIAN, mother of Debbie

"Don't wait for people to ask you questions— just speak up!"

— MARGARET, mother of Andrea

"Never say 'no problem' in response to a request from your boss—that suggests you're being inconvenienced, and that's rude."

— **PAM,** mother of Maya

My mom liked to tell me, "One man's yuck is another man's yum." This was to remind me that just because I didn't like something didn't make it OK for me to disparage someone else's choice.

— **CAIT,** daughter of Barbara

"Always make sure you put a little something aside for yourself, in case you have to leave in a hurry."

— **COOKIE,** mother of Denise

"Don't ever write anything down that you wouldn't want to see on the front page of the *New York Times*."

— **LINDA,** mother of Allison

After my father died, my mother told me not to worry so much. She said she found that the things she spent a lot of time worrying about never happened, and the things that went wrong she never anticipated.

— **SUSAN,** daughter of Sue

My mama always said that if you used "my grandmother died" as an excuse for skipping school, your grandmother would surely die—and I think she meant soon, like *now*. Thank goodness I never tried it, but to this day, before I utter even the smallest white lie, I first sort through it to make sure no innocent person will be ill served.

— ELLEN, daughter of Ardelle

"COUNT YOUR BLESSINGS."

— RUTH, mother of Michael

"You should be three things in life: a devoted friend, an honest person, and a good citizen."

— ELEANOR, mother of Dianne

My mom, in a few words:

"Rise above it."
"Stand up straight."
"Don't hide your light under a bushel."
"Don't bite your nails."
"Have a firm handshake."
"It's *lie* down, not *lay* down."
"Don't sing in your throat."
"Maybe X gets to do it, but you're not X. Would you jump off a bridge just because X did?"
"Keep your head on straight."
"Horrors!"
"I should say."
"You're talking through your hat."
"Don't bear down on your voice."
"It's going to end in a fight, tra la."

— **SIBYL,** daughter of Sybil

> "IF YOU CAN'T HELP IT, DON'T HINDER IT."

— **ALICE,** mother of Dorothy

When I was a boy and I would see scary things in the news, my mother would say to me, "Look for the helpers. You will always find people who are helping."

— **TV personality FRED ROGERS (MR. ROGERS),** son of Nancy

> "DON'T TRUST YOUR SHADOW."

— **ROFA,** mother of Wanda

"ANYTHING WORTH DOING IS WORTH DOING WELL."

— DENISE, mother of Vicki

Mama exhorted her children at every opportunity to "jump at de sun." We might not land on the sun, but at least we would get off the ground.

— Author ZORA NEALE HURSTON, daughter of Lucy Ann

When we were little kids, my sister continually tormented our younger brother. Our mother would say, "Be nice. He'll always be younger than you, but he won't always be smaller."

— ELLEN, daughter of Janice

When my son is trying to take the easy way out of something and asks what he should do, my answer is always, "If you know what's the right thing to do, why would you do anything else?"

— JOAN, mother of Andrew

"If you don't ask, the answer will always be 'no.'"

— PAULINE, mother of Gay

"Act better than you feel."

— JOALICE, mother of Sharon

"Try a new food at least once."

— LOIS LOU, mother of Kirstin

There were five of us, and when we complained there was nothing to do, Mom would shoot back: "'I'm bored?' Read a book, write a poem, or do a puzzle."

— MARGARET, daughter of Joyce

I have often felt that I didn't say enough "Momisms" to my own kids and panicked last year when one was graduating from college and another from high school. Suddenly, my husband and I were empty nesters. I kept saying to him, "I didn't tell them enough!" So I wrote each of my sons a letter explaining how I felt remiss and gave them three tips:

1. Don't drink and drive
2. Put your dish in the dishwasher
3. Call your brother

So, hopefully I did pass along some wisdom over the years, but if not, I figure this is a start.

— **NOREEN,** mother of Michael, Brian, and Daniel

"Somehow things will always work out in the end."

— **JANE,** mother of Ann

"YOU HAVE TO LEARN TO LOVE YOURSELF BEFORE YOU CAN TRULY LOVE SOMEONE ELSE."

— **JENNIFER,** mother of Jessica

"You will never have any fun by saying 'No.' Unless it's 'No, I don't want to go home.'"

— **ELLIE,** mother of Wendy

"FOLLOW YOUR PASSION."

—**JULIA,** mother of Bethanne

Mom always warned us, "Wherever you go, remember that there is someone who knows you, or someone who knows someone who knows you." I'm sure it's because she was always concerned about how our behavior would reflect on her, but the older I get, the more I realize this is true. And that's without Facebook or the twenty-four-hour news cycle.

— LAURA, daughter of Hilda

"If you read, you will find a whole new world out there."

— ELEANOR, mother of Dianne

"Take pride in your work. Let your passions show."

— MARTHA, mother of Sam

"Don't expect one person to give you everything you need. You have to understand yourself well enough to know what your needs are."

— PRISCILLA, mother of Andrew

"Consider the source."

— HELEN, mother of Kip

"You should always leave a place cleaner than when you came."

— ROSEMARY, mother of Victoria

"NEVER LAUGH AT ANYONE'S DREAMS."

— **DOLLY,** mother of Gay

I was a typically self-absorbed teenage girl in the 1960s who fretted over every perceived flaw in my appearance. My freckles were too noticeable. My hair wasn't thick enough. I was too short. My skin was too fair to tan. On and on. I had taken to throwing down copies of *Seventeen* magazine in disgust because I knew I'd never look like its frequent cover girl, Cheryl Tiegs. One day, my very patient mother, who'd had about enough of this self-deprecating nonsense, said, "Just stop it now! You are a beautiful girl and nothing is wrong with you! Even Elizabeth Taylor gets pimples on her butt! Nobody's perfect!" Since then I have never once seen a photo of Elizabeth Taylor without thinking that even one of the most beautiful women in the world was human after all, just like me!

— **CHRIS,** daughter of Nancy

I think my mother learned it from her mother. When she would hear a story of someone getting caught up in someone else's business, my mother would say, "Let the bus driver's mother worry about the bus driver." She meant, "Mind your own business," but no one likes to hear that, especially when you're thoroughly wrapped up in whatever someone else's business might be. But it's an instant "Huh?" to hear the thing about the bus driver. It prompts: "I'm sorry, who is the bus driver? Why are we talking about the bus driver? And who is his mother?" Once you've finally decoded the phrase, you're so distracted by the bus driver (and his mother) that you are no longer involved in whatever (and whoever's) business prompted the remark. My mother was a genius.

— **JENNIFER,** daughter of Jane

My mother's favorite toast:
"Here's to those who are like us and
here's to those who are not.
Here's to those who would like to be
like us and here's to those
who would not—and may the dear
Lord give them a limp so we
know who they are."

— AMY, daughter of Joan

"Don't get old."

— VERA, mother of Audrey

"Make a decision for today. Tomorrow
you can always make another decision."

— MARGARET, mother of Theresa

"IF IT SMELLS, DON'T EAT IT."

— **DEB,** mother of Yanni

GOOD MANNERS & BAD BEHAVIOR

All the stuff your mothers nagged you about all those years? Herein lies the chance to see if she was right.

But you probably know that answer.

"DON'T DO AS I DO. DO AS I SAY DO. WE'RE BUILDING YOUR CHARACTER."

— ETHEL, mother of Sara

"Unless you wear a crown, remove the crest from a sports jacket."

— **POLLY,** mother of David

Mom liked shorthand, I guess, because she always said, "Mind your B, hold your T, do your W, and you will be D." (B is for business, T is for tongue, W for work, and D is for done.)

— **BETSY,** daughter of Rosemary

We moved when I was eleven. I am actually still friends with the first boy I made friends with in the new neighborhood. A couple of months later, our mothers happened to meet.
HIS MOTHER: "Hi. You must be Richard's mother. I'm Jonathon's mother—please call me Muriel."
MY MOTHER: "You may call me Mrs. Katz."

— **RICHARD,** son of Mrs. Katz

Every Catholic kid has heard this when they whine about having to do something they don't want to do: "Offer it up."

— **ALICE,** mother of Mary

"You don't have to like it;
you just have to eat it."

— **CHRIS,** mother of Rhonda

My mom made it hard to get away with bad
behavior—perhaps she remembered all too well.
Every night of my youth when I
went out, her last words as I left were always,
"Wake me up when you get in."

— **SIMON,** son of Suzy

"If only you could be as
nice to your family as
you are to your friends."

— **TESSIE,** mother of Lee

When questioned why she can break one of the Ten Commandments—she's super religious—my mother's reply is always, "I asked God and he gave me permission."

— KIM, daughter of Janet

"LADIES NEVER COMPLAIN OR EXPLAIN."

— CARLOTA, mother of Poo

"Don't salt food other people have made for you before trying it; it hurts the cook's feelings."

— PAM, mother of Maya

"Don't stack dishes at the table."

— PEG, mother of Drew

"YOU CAN'T TELL JUST ONE LIE."

— MARIAN, mother of Pauline

"You should eat like you're dining with the Queen of England."

— ELEANOR, mother of Dianne

It was an automatic "No" if you asked my mother whether one of my friends or cousins could spend the night or eat over while they were standing there next to you.

— JUDY, daughter of Mary

"Always order the cheapest thing on the menu when somebody takes you out to dinner."

— DOROTHY, mother of June

I was about four, and because I was an obedient little girl, I had been pestering my mother for permission to say "shut up." No, she tirelessly repeated, it's not polite and bad manners to boot. But I was equally relentless. One night, as she was giving me a bath, I posed my argument once more, pointing out that all the kids on the block said it.

"Fine," she said, exhausted, "you can say 'shut up.'" I was thrilled; aside from everything else, I'd won my first parental argument. Flush with victory, I began to splash around, and after a few minutes, I had another question for my mom.

"Mama, do you—" I began.

"Shut up!" she shot back.

I burst into tears. And though I had permission, I've never said "shut up" to anyone, ever, since.

— ERIN, daughter of Dorothy

"If you have nothing nice to say, say nothing at all."

— CHERIE, mother of Chris

Our mother didn't want us swearing, so she told us that the worst word she knew was "Oglethorpe." The result was a bunch of children screaming "Oh, Oglethorpe!" at the slightest provocation, thinking we were swearing.

— WENDY, daughter of Ellie

When I was causing trouble, the threat was always: "I'll snatch you bald-headed!"

— SARA, daughter of Ethel

"Act like a lady."

— FAITH, mother of Martha

"Don't make me a young grandmother."

— JANE, mother of Josh

I figured out early as one of seven kids that if I screwed up doing a chore, I wouldn't be asked to do it again. But my mother caught on pretty quick and would always say, "Nothing succeeds like failure." I'm a grandfather now, but I haven't lost my touch— there's still plenty of stuff my wife won't trust me to do around the house.

— BILL, son of Kay

My mom told me that if I didn't behave I would have to be sent to Miss Porter's School, which I thought must be a place for juvenile detention. I was confused to then hear that Jackie Kennedy had gone there and thought she must have really cleaned up her act since her childhood.

— **ROBIN,** daughter of Carol

My mother had a great deal of trouble with me, but I think she enjoyed it.

— Author MARK TWAIN, son of Jane

My mother was not one for swearing, so it was always a little bit of a shock to hear her say when she got angry, "Jesus, Jenny, and the foothills!" She told us that it didn't really have any particular meaning but was a long enough tirade that by the time you finished saying it, you weren't mad anymore.

— MOLLY, daughter of Mary

"BE THE LAST TO ARRIVE AND THE FIRST TO LEAVE."

— MEGAN, mother of Francesca

"I'D RATHER OWE YOU THAN CHEAT YOU OUT OF IT."

— ALICE, mother of Judy

"No fighting, no biting."

— PEG, mother of Peggy

"Never turn down a girl if she asks you to dance."

— SHIRLEY, mother of Richard

"Someone is always watching."

— LOLLY, mother of Dini

"All I want is peace in the house."

— JOAN, mother of Kathryn

Like every mother in the South, mine taught me never to wear white shoes after Labor Day or before Easter, and to "serve from the left and remove from the right" when serving food. While I blithely disregarded her instructions about the sexual propriety that would be required for me to wear white at my wedding, my one attempt to wear white sandals in a sweltering mid-September felt like a rebellion not just against my mother but against the natural order of the world.

When my partner and I get married next September with my mother with us in joyful celebration, both brides will be wearing white dresses, but I don't think white shoes will be an option for me. And at the dinner following, we will of course serve from the left and remove from the right. Times and social norms may change, but some things my mother said will guide me forever.

— **MARGARET,** daughter of Pat

"THIS HURTS ME MORE THAN IT WILL HURT YOU."

— **HILDA,** mother of Helene

> ## "If you're going to eat, make sure you have enough to share."

— CHONG, mother of Benny

I remember as a kid my mother teaching me to stand up when an older woman approaches you in a room.

"How old?" I asked, already a junior etiquette maven. I was taking mental notes.

"An old lady," she said.

I thought that over. "Well, would it hurt someone's feelings if they thought they were too young for me to be standing up?"

The eternal quandary, and one with no real answer. My mother's exasperated catchall was, of course, "Just stand up."

— ERIN, daughter of Dorothy

"Cheerfulness is not a matter of mood—it is an obligation you owe to those around you."

— **MARIAN,** mother of Carla

"CROSS YOUR LEGS AT THE ANKLE— KNEES TOGETHER!"

— **KATHIE,** mother of Hilda

"Always look someone straight in the eye when you shake their hand, and make sure your grip is firm and positive but not overbearing."

— **WINI,** mother of John

When I was in my sneaky teenage stage, I was always trying to fudge scenarios that would be more palatable to my mother so she would let me go out and stay out longer— for instance, "I am going for pizza with so and so (the friend she liked) and then we are going home and watching a movie."

She always knew when I was lying, and would just look at me straight in the eye and say, "Pull the other leg, it's got bells on it."

—CLAIRE, daughter of Jean

WISE WORDS

They're not exactly advice, and they're not quotes from famous philosophers, either. But mothers have an uncanny way of finding the right words for the right time. It must be a perk of the job.

"WALK IN AS IF YOU OWN THE PLACE."

— **PEG,** mother of Margaret

My mother said I must always be intolerant of ignorance but understanding of illiteracy. That some people, unable to go to school, were more educated and more intelligent than college professors.

— Poet MAYA ANGELOU, daughter of Vivian

"You know what you know; find out what they know."

— LYNN, mother of Linda

"Always remember that you are not better than anyone else, and no one is better than you."

— SANNY, mother of Tom

"A lady closes her drapes at night and opens them first thing in the morning."

— KATHIE, mother of Hilda

"Never be too happy or too sad" was always one of my favorites from mom. Every time I would get really excited about something, she would lay that one on me so I would rein it in. She was right, by the way.

— NANCY, daughter of Mary

"Sing something that matters."

— GLORIA, mother of singer Amy Grant

"If you have to tell someone you are, chances are you are not."

— **BURKIE,** mother of J.

"You should always have the Bible on your iPad, 'cause you never know when you'll need to call on the Lord."

— MARGARET,
mother of journalist Jonathan Capehart

"It's a great life if you don't weaken!"

— **FELICE,** mother of Shelley

"It's good to look at something different."

— **DOLORES,** mother of Gary

ON THE SUBJECT OF TYPING:

"You're going to summer school to learn how to type. Then you can go to New York City and get a great job as a secretary at Time-Life."
— DOROTHY, mother of Erin

"Learn typing and stenography and stay with it. That way you'll meet a nice husband."
— NAN, mother of Nancy

"learn to type, but don't tell anybody."
— LEIGH, mother of Gina

"NEVER LEARN TO TYPE."
— PHYLLIS, mother of Laura

On originality in the arts:
"There is no such thing
as an original thought."

— **MARGARET,** mother of Andrew

"IT'S ONLY GOOD
WHEN BOTH SIDES
ARE HAPPY."

— **LEA,** mother of Lizzz

"Show me your friends and
I'll tell you who you are."

— **MIMI,** mother of Joni

My mother started saying this to us when we first got our drivers' licenses, but I find now—and I'm a mother myself—that it's still great advice: "Watch out for the men in blue!"

— **ELLEN,** daughter of Sally

"Never discuss politics or religion with friends."

— **LILLIAN,** mother of Diane

Whenever we would say, "Everyone is doing it" —whatever "it" was— my mother would respond, "Be the engine and not the caboose."

— **JANE,** daughter of Omerine

"Never stress out to make yourself sick."

— **MARY,** mother of Della

"We don't hate."

— **JERRI,** mother of Lindy

"DON'T FORGET: OTHER PEOPLE DON'T KNOW EVERYTHING THAT YOU KNOW."

— **ANN,** mother of Lynn & daughter of Ann

My mom has a way of cutting herself off when she's about to comment on something someone is doing that she doesn't approve of. Suddenly she'll stop and say, "But I'm not on that committee."

— **MARTHA,** daughter of Beverly

"If you wait until you have enough money to have children, you'll never have them."

— **ALICE,** mother of Barb

*My mother fled Germany just ahead of the Nazis, though
some of her family—including her own mother—were not so
fortunate. Recalling the things she used to say, I realize now
that they are all about survival, one way or another . . .*

"Don't tell anybody anything, unless it is necessary, and think on it first!"

"Sticks and stones can break your bones— but silence can break your heart."

"Live in the present, look forward to the future, and refuse to be dominated by the past."

"There is no such thing as love. There is only proof of love."

"If we fill our hours with regrets of yesterday and with worries of tomorrow, we have no today in which to be thankful."

— HERTHA, mother of Tina

"Save love letters. They continue to bring
joy as the years ramble on."

— **MARTHA,** mother of Sam

When I was five years old, my mother always told
me that happiness was the key to life. When I went
to school, they asked me what I wanted to be when
I grew up. I wrote down "happy." They told me
I didn't understand the assignment, and I told them
they didn't understand life.

— Musician **JOHN LENNON,** son of Julia

In circumstances where you had hurt yourself or
were sad about something, Mom always said, "It'll
all be gone by the time you're married." We never
understood that, but we're all married now, and she
doesn't say that anymore. So maybe she was right.

— **KAT,** daughter of Ruth

"Every child has to eat a peck of dirt."

— **VERA,** mother of Audrey

Mom's Yiddish version of "You can't take it with you":
"There are no pockets in a shroud."

— **LIZ,** daughter of Judith

When I lost my first—and only—run for elective office (to the New York City Council) and I was particularly sad for several months, Mom said, "Liz, you have no sense of humor—you must always, always maintain your sense of humor!"
She also told me,
"Never hesitate to tell the truth, never give in, and never give up."

— LIZ, daughter of Congresswoman Bella Abzug

"We mothers are learning to mark our mothering success by our daughters' lengthening flight."

— Author and feminist
LETTY COTTIN POGREBIN,
mother of Abigail and Robin

"It's better to have it and not need it than need it and not have it."

— MERRILL, mother of Sarah

"Ya damned if ya do and ya damned if ya don't!"

— BARBARA, mother of Eddie

"If everyone's troubles were thrown in a pile, you would scramble after your own."

— MIDDY, mother of Buffy

"It's important to know you're happy *while* you're happy—otherwise you realize how good you had it only when it's gone."

— SHIRLEY, mother of Alix

"Be nice to your sister. She will be your best friend in life." (And she is.)

— EDYTHE, mother of Deborah

"Always check the back of a man's shoes—you can tell if he's rich or poor."

— ESPERANZA, mother of Diana

My mother always said that everyone should be required to write an autobiography of their lives.

— Actor DIANE KEATON,
daughter of Dorothy

"THERE'S NO GREAT LOSS WITHOUT SOME SMALL GAIN."

— LOIS, mother of Ellen

"Never talk about anything important after 10 P.M."

— MARTHA, mother of Michael

"It is not how old you are—but how you are old."

— HERTHA, mother of Tina

"It's nice to be nice."

— ALICE, mother of Sheila

"Don't let the perfect be the enemy of the good."

— SANDRA, mother of Nichole, invoking Voltaire

"You're as happy as you make up your mind to be."

— LOUISE, mother of Kathy

"Hope for the best, prepare for the worst."

— RITA, mother of Lisa

"Inch by inch, life's a cinch. Yard by yard, life is hard."

— **ANN**, mother of Amelia

"Kids lie quicker than a cat can wink his eye."

— **ZADDIE**, mother of Chimere

"NO WOMAN LIKES A HANDSOME DUMMY."

— **DASHANA**, mother of Elijah

"A leopard never changes its spots" was said over and over to remind me that people don't change. With every new boyfriend disappointment, job challenge, and life lesson, I was reminded that people don't change—you do.

— **LORI**, daughter of Gigi

Whenever I was upset because I'd been teased at school, or because I didn't fit in, or because I wanted something that "everyone else" had, my mom would say: "Wouldn't the world be boring if everyone was exactly the same?" The older I get, the more I realize this is a beautiful truth.

— **EMILY,** daughter of Teresa

At the dinner table with five daughters, my mom's constant reminder was, "She who eats the fastest, gets the mostest."

— **KAT,** daughter of Ruth

"Save money; disaster is coming."

— **GIT JING,** mother of William

If I were faced with a challenge or a difficult activity that worried me, Mother's final words as I left the house were always, "Do it pretty."

— **DOROTHY,** daughter of Alice

Mothers are fonder than fathers of their children because they are more certain they are their own.

— **Philosopher ARISTOTLE,** son of Phaestis

"Always be happy for another person. Their success doesn't take anything away from you."

— ELLIE, mother of Wendy

Whenever I was being judgmental of someone, my mother said: "It's *his* journey."

— ERIC, son of Cecelia

"God gives the back for the burden."

— JUNE DENISE, mother of Jim

"Pay attention to what he does, not what he says."

— FRAN, mother of Ann

Seems every holiday or celebration or wherever food was being served, everyone would worry— would there be enough? After a while, my mother would always just cut the decision short with, "When it's gone, it's gone!"

— SUZY, daughter of Tessie

When my mother ponders her remaining years at her job, she says: "I'm here to drink milk, not to count cows."

— SONIA, daughter of Satyra

"TAKE NOTES."

— Playwright **PHOEBE EPHRON,** mother of Nora

"Make your mess your message."

— **LUCIMARIAN,**
mother of TV journalist Robin Roberts

"EVERYTHING IS COPY."

— Author and director **NORA EPHRON,**
daughter of Phoebe

"What's funnier than people?"

— **HAZEL,** mother of Hope

I still use my mother's expressions, and I think of her (and sound like her) when I use them. When I was young and I got upset with the clothes I had on for an event, I would storm around the house, complaining about how stupid I looked. Mother would say, "Smile and no one will notice."

— **DOROTHY,** daughter of Alice

"IT'S NICE TO BE RICH, NO DISGRACE TO BE POOR— BUT IT'S DAMN INCONVENIENT AT TIMES."

— **BROOKS,** mother of Pamela

"Make sure you let your children know how much you love them every day, and when you leave for work communicate how important your career is to you, and how much you love working."

— **PRISCILLA,** mother of Peter

"Just because a man is a good dancer doesn't mean you'll get to spend the rest of your life dancing."

— **HATTIE,** mother of Virginia

"Who don't hear shall feel."

— **LINDA,** mother of Raymond

This was always my mom's warning when she thought I might get into trouble with the wrong crowd: "Peter pays for Paul, and Paul pays for all."

— **LENA,** mother of Tiffany

QUESTIONABLE WISDOM

?

Some would call it crazy talk. And yet, and yet . . . there's often a nugget of *good* crazy there. Enough that we keep listening, right?

"MAY IS A GOOD MONTH FOR A FACE LIFT."

— **LEE,** mother of Lesley

My mother told me on the way to a fancy party, "Remember, the first millionaire is the hardest to catch. After that the second and third are easy."

— **Author KAYLIE JONES,** daughter of Gloria

> ## *"Nothing good happens after midnight."*

— **EDITH,** mother of Dick

"Don't think so much!" my mother was always saying. "You're going to get depressed, and you'll get big wrinkles on the bridge of your nose." She was not joking—and, viewed in a certain light, she was right.

— **CHRISTINE,** daughter of Anne

"To avoid bad luck, never let anyone sit on your matrimonial bed. For example, if your mother-in-law sits there, family problems will break up your marriage."

— **ESPERANZA,** mother of Diana

I remember the first time I heard my mother say this, and I quickly incorporated it into my own repertoire. My parents had moved to Florida, and I had called in for our weekly chat.

"How's everything?" I asked. "How's the weather?"

"Well," my mother replied, "we're OK, but there's a terrible thing going around, and everybody seems to be sick. There's hardly anyone down at the pool."

"Really? What is it?" I asked.

"*Pffft*. Well, Myra Saperstein down on the third floor says it's some kind of crazy flu from Singapore. But, you know her: 'Myra Saperstein, AAD.' She thinks she knows everything."

"AAD? What's that?" I asked.

"Myra Saperstein, Also A Doctor."

I howled, because not only was it funny but, I thought, she should talk! My mother was AAD, AAEsq, and AAPhD herself.

— **ELYSE,** daughter of Hilda

> ## "No one promised you tomorrow."

— ISABEL, mother of Karen

My mother always mentored me in business, and though she's never technically been a part of my company, I've always said she's the brains behind the entire operation. Her warning about charging too much or being too greedy has always been the same, and it's a good one: "Pigs get slaughtered."

— LIZZZ, daughter of Lea

"Dogs that bark don't bite."

— ROFA, mother of Wanda

My mother often mutters under her breath, especially now that she's gotten older. But every time I say to her, "Why are you always talking to yourself?" she'll zing back, "I like to talk to smart people."

— DIANE, daughter of Fae

"Marry someone good-looking. If you don't have any money tucked under the bed, at least you have something handsome to look at in the morning."

— **MARY,** mother of Nan

"Eat your crusts if you want your hair to curl."

— **MARGIE,** mother of Margaret

My mother's explanation for why my sisters and I take after my grandmother in the kitchen—and she, well, not so much: "Cooking skips a generation."

— **ELISA,** daughter of Jo

"Whistling girls and cackling hens always come to some bad end."

— **AGNES,** mother of Sis

"Save everything. Even hats will come back."

— **LEE,** mother of Lesley

"When you sit next to a man at a dinner party, ask him questions about himself. Do not talk about yourself. He will leave the table thinking you were a great dinner partner."

— **OLIVE,** mother of Olive

"If you're using
a public coatroom,
always button or zip up
your coat so someone
else's is easier to steal."

— MARY, mother of Betsy

Whenever I'm tired:
"Have a drink.
You'll perk right up!"

— ANNE, mother of Emma

"Relationships are like
hailing a cab: one goes by,
you hail the next one."

— REGINA, mother of Liz

"WEAR A SWEATER,
I'M COLD."

— ANNE, mother of Karen

"Eat every kernel in
your rice bowl or your wife
will be ugly."

— GIT JING, mother of William

"Never stand if you can
sit and never sit if you
can lie down."

— BROOKS, mother of Pamela

"If you wash your windows,
your whole house will
look clean."

— DORIS, mother of Nancy

As a teenager, whenever
I left the house my mother
always said, "Don't get in
a fight." It always made
me laugh because I *never*
got in a fight, and if I did,
I knew I would be the one
to get beat up. But she
always said it. Maybe part
of the reason I never *did*
get in a fight was due to
her insistence.

— CAREY, son of Ellen

Whenever I got sick, my
mother's usual wisdom
was: "It came; it'll go away."

— RUTH, daughter of Hazel

"It's the sugar that gives you a hangover,
not the alcohol."

— **BARBARA,** mother of Michelle

"Clarity is power."

— **MARGARET,** mother of Alexis

"Don't get above your raisin'."

— **CANDY,** mother of Cris

My mom, meaning it as encouragement, said to my
sister when she'd call during exam week in
veterinary school, whining: "Even if they're crucifying
you upside down, it'll be over in three days."

— **MARY,** daughter of Celia

*"If someone hits you,
hit them back."*

— **CLAIRE,** mother of Stephan

According to my mother, there are several words one should never say or use (even in writing), including: *drapes, sales rep, limo, tux, couch, assistant, gorgeous, restroom, luggage, wealthy.*

It was always to be: *curtains, salesman, limousine, tuxedo, sofa, secretary, beautiful, bathroom, suitcase, rich,* instead.

— **JOHN,** son of Wini

"Don't put your shoes on the table— it's bad luck!"

— **ROSE,** mother of Stella

"Never buy someone a pair
of shoes or they will walk
out of your life."

— CHUNG, mother of Irene

My mother always had
the most annoying saying
when it rained on vacation:
"We'll just have to make
our own sunshine!"

— HOLLY, mother of Corky

"Life would be a lot
simpler if people didn't
have to eat."

— BERTA, mother of Katrina

"I MAY NOT
ALWAYS BE RIGHT,
BUT I AM NEVER
WRONG."

— BOBBIE, mother of Cathie

I think the first time I heard
this we were watching *Dirty
Dancing* or something with
Patrick Swayze or some
other handsome type. Me
being the young'un, I either
shot my mother a look
when she admired the male
lead or said something along
the lines of, "But Mom,
you're married!" To which
she responded, "It doesn't
matter where you get your
appetite, as long as you eat
at home."

— KRISTINA, daughter of Sandy

"It's as easy to fall in
love with a rich man
as a poor one."

— CATHIE, mother of Brenda

"I always thought that
growing up was overrated."

— JANE, mother of Diana

"If you shave above your
legs, you'll get cancer."

— JACQUI, mother of Jen

My mother said that the number of snowfalls in a season is determined by the day of the month of the first snowfall. So if it's on December 15, there will be fifteen snowfalls. How do you know what's enough to be called a snowfall? "Why, enough for a rabbit to make tracks in the woods, of course."

— **HOPE,** daughter of Hazel

The cure-all—
whether you're sick,
on a diet, crying,
or waiting for the
phone to ring:
"Drink some water."

— **JOAN,** mother of Sarah

MOM LEARNED IT ALL FROM GRANDMA

It had to start somewhere! And if wisdom skipped a generation in some families, it looks like Grandma has always been happy to step in.

"WHAT DO YOU EXPECT FROM A PIG BUT A GRUNT?"

— **ALICE,** grandmother of Mary

"You have to work with what you have
to get what you want."

— **FRANCES,** grandmother of Tim

"Don't spit on my back and tell me it's raining."

— **MARY,** great-grandmother of Ilene

On chastity:

**"A woman can't be too careful. . . .
She shouldn't even completely
trust her own nightgown."**

— **ANTONIA,** grandmother of David

At the commencement of any recipe, my
grandmother said: "First, you take out your pan."

— **KATHRYN,** granddaughter of Mary

When we said something was too hard:
"What's easy? Easy is peeing in the bathtub."
— ILENE, great-granddaughter of Mary

"Dishes don't get dirtier overnight."
— CAROL, grandmother of Wesley

*"Sing before breakfast,
cry before night."*

— HATTIE, grandmother of Meredith

"Having a toddler is like having a permanently
drunk houseguest."
— EMILY, grandmother of Megan

"Don't whistle at night because it will attract bats."
— SU-YU, grandmother of Jating

"YOU WILL CRY BLOOD WHEN I DIE."

— CECELIA,
grandmother of Denise

"Love many; trust few."

— FLORENCE,
grandmother of Nancy

"A little powder and paint makes you feel what you ain't."

— FRANCES,
grandmother of Ilene

"If they come for a visit, they do me one favor; if they don't come, they do me two."

— ANTONIA,
grandmother of David

Grandma always said, "Never forget to use your best tool in the kitchen." She quickly would take the side of her hand to remove the pancake batter from a bowl instead of reaching for a spatula.

— RHONDA,
granddaughter of Gin

"If you put it back in the same place every time, it would be there when you looked for it."

— GIGI,
grandmother of Kathleen

"PINK MAKES THE BOYS WINK."

— AGNES, grandmother of Anne

Grandma could be incredibly critical, especially
when it came to interior decorating and clothing.
But she was not one to voice an opinion beyond
a raised eyebrow and the simple phrase,
"It's not *my* taste."
But perhaps my favorite is, "Be careful going."
This is what my grandmother told me whenever
I left her apartment to head for home on the
subway to Manhattan (from Brooklyn) after
our weekly visits. I now say it to my husband
whenever he's leaving the house.
I can't help myself.

— **ERIC,** grandson of May

"When poverty comes in
the window, love goes
out the door."

— **MABEL,** grandmother of Brad

This fashion advice, originally offered by my
grandmother to my mom, used to make my mother
roll her eyes. When my mom was growing up in the
1970s (when it wasn't cool to dress conservatively),
she would model a funky skirt or a pair of bell bottoms,
and no matter what it was, my grandma would always
say, "You know what that would look good with?
A nice white blouse."
Of course my mom thought that was the lamest thing,
but now I find she sometimes says it to me:
"Everything looks good with a nice white blouse."

— LOGAN, daughter of Patty, granddaughter of Sue

My Italian grandmother, on sweating the small stuff:
"If you let your feet get stubbed on every rock on the
road, the rocks won't mind, but you'll arrive home
with badly injured feet."

— DAVID, grandson of Antonia

"As long as you have a hot
meal on the table and eat
together as a family each
night you'll never be poor."

— FLORENCE, grandmother of Tim

My grandmother was continually frustrated that I didn't seem to be progressing toward marriage. She would always ask me if I'd met someone yet whom I liked better than myself.

— **MARJORY,** granddaughter of Bella

ACKNOWLEDGMENTS

A huge thanks to Cathy Grier, who buttonholed me one night and pointed out that I quoted my mother more often than I ever would have thought. And to my Abrams family, who all immediately burned up their office email with tales of their own mothers the minute they heard about the idea for this book—they "got it" right away, and knew folks everywhere would also enjoy sharing their own memories (this means you, Michael Jacobs, Mary Wowk, Steve Tager, Deb Aaronson, Merle Browne, and the rest of you). Always my thanks to my stalwart and delightful editor, David Cashion, my relentless publicist, Marisa Dobson, and hats off for the incredible help and humor of designer Rachel Willey.

And of course it wouldn't be a book without the input and memories from all the men and women within these pages: fathers, mothers, sons, and daughters themselves. Some will share this book with their moms—and many of us will hold it dear as a book full of memories.

ABOUT THE AUTHOR

Erin McHugh is a former publishing executive and the award-winning author of more than twenty books of trivia, history, children's titles, and more, including *One Good Deed: 365 Days of Trying to Be Just a Little Bit Better*. She splits her time between New York City and South Dartmouth, Massachusetts.

She is the daughter of Dorothy Kavanaugh McHugh.